Faith Begins @ Home
FAMILY

Whether it's connecting with your kids on a genuine level or diffusing conflict in the home, Mark Holmen offers solid advice based on his years of ministry to families. This little book offers a great recipe for harmony in the home.

Jim Daly
President, Focus on the Family

Mark Holman is leading a movement of God across the world to reestablish the home as the primary place where faith is lived and nurtured. This booklet comes at a time when parents have a deep desire to see their children learn to walk with God and grow in faith. Every parent needs this resource.

Jim Burns, Ph.D.
President, HomeWord
Author, *Confident Parenting* and *Teaching Your Children Healthy Sexuality*

Every generation benefits from leaders who challenge it to excellence. Mark's life experiences have equipped him to be an insightful leader who calls readers to action. His message is powerful and simple: We need more "faith at home." I hope to hear Mark proclaim this message for many years to come. I thoroughly endorse and support him in his vision to establish "faith at home" in households around the world!

Ken Canfield, Ph.D.
Founder, National Center for Fathering

Once again Mark delivers with another Faith @ Home resource. You must read this thought-provoking and practical resource for your family. The segments in each chapter entitled "Faith @ Home Family Insight" give great practical advice and wisdom for parents. It can't be missed!

Craig Jutila
Author, *Faith and the Modern Family*
CEO Empowered Living
www.whowillyouempower.com

Mark Holmen

Author, *Faith Begins at Home* and Founder of Faith @ Home Ministries

Faith Begins
@Home
FAMILY

Regal

From Gospel Light
Ventura, California, U.S.A.

Published by Regal
From Gospel Light
Ventura, California, U.S.A.
www.regalbooks.com
Printed in the U.S.A.

Library of Congress Cataloging-in-Publication Data
Holmen, Mark.
Faith begins @ home family / Mark Holmen.
pages cm
ISBN 978-0-8307-6973-5 (trade paper)
Families—Religious life. I. Title. II. Title: Faith begins at
home family.
BV4526.3.H67 2014
248.4—dc23
2013027672

Rights for publishing this book outside the U.S.A. or in
non-English languages are administered by Gospel Light
Worldwide, an international not-for-profit ministry. For additional
information, please visit www.glww.org, email info@glww.org,
or write to Gospel Light Worldwide, 1957 Eastman Avenue,
Ventura, CA 93003, U.S.A.

To order copies of this book and other Regal products in bulk
quantities, please contact us at 1-800-446-7735.

I would like to dedicate this book to our
Lord and Savior Jesus Christ and all the incredible
families He has given me the chance to serve during
my years in ministry. I have been blessed by your
faithfulness in times of trial, your steadfastness in times
of uncertainty, your joy in the midst of pain,
your adaptability in an ever-changing world and
your unending commitment to following Christ
no matter what you face as a family. I appreciate the
stories you share with me at seminars, via social media
and personal emails. Thank you for sharing how
God is working through your faithfulness to be a
Faith @ Home Family—God will use these to positively
impact thousands of families all over the world.
Keep them coming and I'll keep sharing them
all for the glory of God!

Contents

Introduction

I loved the *Cosby Show* and I still find myself enjoying it today whenever I can find an episode to watch. I also like television shows like *Blue Bloods, Modern Family* and *Castle* because they take you into the lives of families and you get to watch how they wrestle through an issue or development. While the Cosbys aren't a "real" family, the issues they dealt with were certainly "real time" issues. Many times, after watching an episode, I would find myself saying, "That was a great way to handle that situation."

This booklet is going to read like a television show where each chapter will be an episode that will introduce you to a family and a modern day issue they encountered. While the names of the family members in each episode have been changed, the topics and issues addressed in each episode are based on real experiences I en-countered in my 20-plus years of ministry working with families. My hope and prayer is that each one of these episodes will serve as an example of how you can bring Christ and Christ-like living into these modern realities.

1

A Rocky Road

Jim was out of town on a business trip when the phone rang at 1:30 AM. "Are you awake, honey?" his wife Trish said on the other end of the line. "I need you to be fully awake because what our daughter needs to share with you is going to need your full and complete attention."

Jim and Trish were a strong Christian couple who had raised their daughter, Jenny, in a strong Christian household. Church was a normal part of life for them along with faith talk in the home, prayer and Christian music. Jenny was sixteen and had been pretty much a straight A student all the way through her years attending a Christian school. Jenny had never shown any signs of slipping or engaging in any form of misbehavior. The worst thing she had ever done was to go TP'ing! Just a couple of years earlier Jenny had gone on a youth retreat where she had made a commitment to purity and remaining pure until she got married. She proudly wore a purity ring on her ring finger as a symbolic reminder of that commitment. Jenny's first boyfriend, DJ, had even been a good experience for the family as he was also a Christian who came from a good Christian family. By every indicator, Jim and Trish were doing it right, and Jenny was on track doing life God's way with good Christian friends and a Christian boyfriend alongside her.

"Jim there is something Jenny needs to tell you and you are gonna need to be sitting down for this as this is going to be very hard for you to hear." Jim braced himself and his daughter got on the phone and confessed that she had broken her purity commitment by having sex with her boyfriend. Jim was crushed. The purity commitment had created such a powerful bond between his daughter and him. He had picked out her ring and proudly gave it to her after she made her commitment. He was looking forward to one day receiving that ring back from her on her wedding day as she put on her wedding ring. Jim had even befriended DJ and was excited about him because he was a Christian kid from a Christian family. They had gone to church together and texted prayers for each other. Jim trusted Jenny and DJ and thought his trust was well placed based on the way both of them were committed to following Christ. So Jim was devastated and found himself wondering, *How could this be happening?* He was hurt, angry, disappointed, disillusioned and lost for words. Jenny awaited his response over the phone, "I don't know what to say. I'm very disappointed, angry and hurt and I need some time to figure this out. Thanks for telling me but this is really hard for me right now. We will talk about this more when I get home."

Jim's world had come crashing down around him. His daughter was clearly broken and had hit rock bottom. He knew she needed him but he didn't know what to think, say or do. Giving her worldly punishments or consequences seemed hollow at this point. He could tell her she was done dating until she was 21 but would that really be the answer? He could take her out of the private school she was attending but that didn't seem like the best idea either. He was mad and he wanted to do something because that's what guys do. Not knowing what to do Jim did something he wasn't even sure he wanted to do. He turned to Scripture. He didn't know where to turn because it's not like there is a specific place to go on how to deal with a teenager who has broken her commitment not to have sex before marriage. So even though he knew the Bible well, at this moment he blindly opened it just looking for anything that might give him some sort of direction. And God lead him to Galatians 6:1-2.

• •

Faith@Home Family Insight

When worldly things happen don't turn to worldly answers; seek Godly answers!

• •

Brothers, if someone is caught in a sin, you who are spiritual should restore him gently. But watch yourself, or you also may be tempted. Carry each other's burdens, and in this way you will fulfill the law of Christ (Galatians 6:1-2).

The passage confronted Jim in a way he was ill-prepared for and yet he knew instantly what he had to do. His daughter had been caught in sin and it was now his job to restore her gently. It didn't say punish her instantly, confront her angrily, humiliate her publicly or beat her down emotionally. It said, "restore [her] gently" and as you do, "watch carefully or you also may be tempted." He needed to help "carry her burdens." And, as if that wasn't enough, Jim was also convicted that he needed not only to restore his daughter gently, but also DJ.

That entire night and during the flight home the next day, Jim searched God's Word on how to "restore gently." Through that journey God revealed to Jim a five-step restoration process for how he could do that with Jenny and DJ.

- Step 1–Acknowledge/name the sin and the damage it has done. Leave no stone unturned. Get it all out.
- Step 2–Help those caught in sin cast their burdens onto Jesus or they will carry the weight of them forever.
- Step 3–Fully recognize and embrace the reality that the sin has been forgiven and the weight of it is gone.

- Step 4–Discuss and develop a plan/strategy for how to "sin no more" and ways in which to "flee temptation."
- Step 5–Celebrate the new life that has been given. Party, be happy and be filled with joy again. Life is good when you have been restored!

When Jim got home, no one knew what to expect. He embraced his daughter and after comforting her he simply said he needed to talk to his wife so they could collectively decide what they were going to do next. Jim shared with Trish the journey he had been on that led to the five-step restoration process. Then, with Trish's help, they developed a plan for how they would enact the restoration process. A few days later, on a Sunday morning, Jim woke his daughter, Jenny, and said, "Put on some sweats and sneakers because we are going to go for a ride and a walk." This had never happened before, but Jenny simply got ready and they jumped into the car. Jim drove to a nearby park. On the way Jim explained how God had led him to Galatians 6:1-2 and that he wanted to lead Jenny through a restoration process. She agreed to the plan. When they got to the park Jim went to the trunk and pulled out a backpack filled with rocks. He placed it on his daughter's back and then said, "Let's go."

The park had a two-mile trail that was sharply uphill and went to a place where there was a lookout with a cross. As they began the walk Jim told Jenny what the first step of the journey was going to be about. "Jenny, I know you are carrying a big burden as a result of what you have done. The backpack you are carrying is not light because the burdens you are carrying are not light. So as we walk, let's name those burdens and see what happens."

Jim pulled out a list of ways that he and his wife had been hurt by what Jenny had done and he started sharing them with her and as he did, Jenny began to cry because these were not easy things for her to hear. But as he talked, Jim did something unexpected; he reached into her backpack and cast a stone into the woods. He continued to share one burden after another and after each one, he would cast another stone into the woods. With each burden shared, and each stone cast into the woods, the backpack got a little lighter.

When they reached the lookout where the cross was located, Jim turned to Jenny and said, "Sweetie, I'm done. I've unloaded all the burdens your mom and I have because of what you have done. I know that wasn't easy for you to hear, but now, as you can tell by the weight of the backpack, some of the burden has been lifted. You still have some weight in that backpack and it's because you have your own burdens you need to get rid of." He then told Jenny that he was going to give her some private time to do whatever she needed to do to offload the remaining burdens she had on her heart and mind that were weighing her down. He instructed her to take some time to name them and as she did, she should cast the remaining rocks down at the foot of the cross. Jenny walked to the cross and with tears rolling down her eyes, she slowly reached in and pulled one rock after another out of the backpack and tossed it down at the foot of the cross. When she was done she came back to where her dad was sitting and they embraced. Jim simply reminded her of the story of the woman caught in adultery and said to Jenny, "No one is here to condemn you anymore. Not your mom. Not me. And not your God. Now leave this life of sin and go and sin no more."

Jim then placed the empty backpack on his back and the two walked down from the cross. Jim used this opportunity to discuss what they needed to do so that Jenny could steer clear of the pitfall into which she had fallen. In this discussion many things surfaced that became good changes to make for them as a family. In many ways those changes would bring them back to a more God-honoring lifestyle at home. As Jim later shared, "It wasn't like we had become a bad family, but we had begun to slip a little and this series of events brought us back to a more God-honoring place."

Yet there was still one more step in the restoration process—a surprise awaiting Jenny. When Jim and Jenny got home, Trish had prepared Jenny's favorite meal as a celebration dinner. Trish shared, "I wanted her to know that I was ready to move forward as well, so I used the love language I have to show her that." When Jenny saw all that her mom was making she was moved again to tears and simply said, "I can't believe you did all this for me after what I have put you through." Trish wrapped her arms around Jenny and whispered to her, "I didn't do this for you. I did it for us. We are going to be okay. In fact we are going to be better than before! I will always love you. Now help me finish making all of this because we have a guest coming!" "A guest?" Jenny asked. Who's coming?" Trish simply responded, "You will just have to wait and see."

Jim departed and went to pick up DJ. He had called DJ's parents and explained what he wanted to do so that they didn't think he was going to kill their teenage son! Jim then repeated the same process with DJ because God had laid it on his heart that DJ needed to be restored gently as well. DJ had texted Jim numerous times confessing his sin to Jim and how badly he felt for betraying his trust and confidence. As DJ and Jim began their walk up to the lookout, Jim didn't hold back in telling DJ all the ways he had hurt his daughter, his wife and him as well. But as he talked, Jim did the same as he had for Jenny and took a rock out of the backpack and cast it into the woods. "In many ways I was tougher on DJ than my daughter because I felt he had taken something from her and from us and I needed him to know that. Yet I made sure I also did so as gently as I could so I wasn't the one sinning. I just threw those rocks a little harder!" In many ways, the walk was as important for Jim as it was for DJ as it enabled him to share things he needed to get off his chest.

When they got to the cross Jim also invited DJ to spend some time at the cross casting down any remaining burdens he had at the foot of the cross. DJ tossed one rock after another at the foot of the cross and when he was done, DJ and Jim had a time of prayer together.

On the walk down, Jim used this time as an opportunity to discuss with DJ changes that would be implemented so as to avoid future temptations and DJ added some of his own ideas as well. They got in the car and Jim proceeded to take DJ to their home. He was their surprise dinner guest. Jenny hadn't known if DJ would ever be welcome in their home again. Together they all enjoyed the celebration feast that Trish had prepared.

• •

Faith@Home Family Insight

Life is going to happen in every family. Bubbles are going to get burst. Feelings hurt. Things are not going to turn out in the way you expected, and disappointment is going to happen. We live in a world where for some premarital sex is considered a normal part of life. Yet we all have God's ideal in mind that involves carefully navigating our kids through life in a way that keeps them from engaging in premarital sex. We do everything in our power to protect, guide and empower them to avoid entanglements and situations that lead to sex. And don't get me wrong, some make it through, and for that we say praise the Lord! Yet for others, God's ideal can be crushed by the reality that sin still happens in spite of our very best efforts to prevent it.

• •

Hopefully, what you have learned from the very real story of Jim, Trish, Jenny and DJ is the fact that the ideal does not have to be crushed by sin, but through God's grace, the ideal can be restored! Yes, sin is real, but so is restoration! Restoration can happen and out of death can come new life. A modern Faith@Home family is not a perfect family where no sin exists. Instead a modern Faith@Home family is a family that actively engages in restoration and carrying each other's burdens.

The Rest of the Story

A few months after the restoration Sunday experience, Jim noticed that his daughter was not wearing her purity ring. He asked his wife Trish why that was the case. She answered, "She doesn't think she can wear it anymore because of what she did with DJ." At the next opportunity Jim talked with his daughter about her thoughts. While Jenny understood that she had been forgiven, she didn't fully understand that she had been restored and that meant she was pure again. She was free to begin wearing the ring again. This conversation opened up another wonderful Faith@Home moment for Jim and Jenny which led to her wearing the ring again. And finally, if you were to talk to Jim, Trish and Jenny today they would actually say that their relationship and life together as a family is better as a result of that event. While they wouldn't want to relive it, they testify to the fact that they are a better family as a result.

DISCUSSION QUESTIONS

1. Did you ever go through a restoration process for something you did as a child/teenager? What impact did it have in your life?
2. Is there anything you are hanging onto about which you have never completely felt restored? How would going through a restoration process have helped you?
3. Review the steps for restoration that Jim identified from Scripture. Which step was the most meaningful for you? Which step would be the hardest for you to initiate in your family?
4. Is there something that needs to be restored in your child? What will be your plan?

2

70 x 7

Tom and Sheila were relatively active church attendees with two teenage sons. Tom was a former high school and college athlete and his wife, Sheila, enjoyed working out and playing sports as well. It didn't come as a surprise to either of them that their sons would become athletes too. Each year was a flurry of activity as the boys went from one sports season to another and each of their sons seemed to excel in their respective sport. Jordan, their eldest, was the quieter of the two boys, yet most could see that Nathan was the more gifted athlete. He excelled primarily because he wanted to beat his older brother! Both of the boys attended Sunday School and youth group, and both got good grades. Everything seemed to be on solid ground for them as a family.

When Jordan went to high school, he went out for the same sports teams he had been involved in as a junior high student, but while he made the teams, in this much larger high school environment, he now found himself on the second and third strings which kept him from playing most games. During this same time Nathan was excelling on his junior high teams and he was already getting the attention of the high school coaches. Many times Jordan would hear his high school coach say, "That brother of yours is really quite the athlete. Can't wait till he's here playing for us!" While Tom and Sheila attended both of their son's games, most of their time and attention focused on talking about Nathan and his games because he was playing while Jordan was not.

Jordan began disengaging from some of his longtime athletic friends and instead began hanging out with some new friends. Neither Tom nor Sheila thought much of it. They could see that their son was looking for something else from life than sports. Since his grades were still good, they weren't overly concerned even when he began to disengage from his church youth group. As Tom told me, "Heck, I quit going to youth group when I was his age, so I didn't think much of it."

When Jordan became a junior in high school, Nathan entered as a freshman and unlike his older brother he not only made the sports teams, he was starting for most of them. Most weekends consisted of going to Nathan's games. Tom and Sheila did not know that Jordan was spending most of the game time doing drugs with his new friends. Over the course of the next year this continued, Jordan went further and further into drug use while his family was further and further engaged in Nathan's athletic endeavors. Finally, the drug use began to affect Jordan's grades and behavior and it became just a matter of time before his parents discovered the truth.

"Hello Tom, this is the principal of your son's school and I need you to come to my office at your earliest convenience. There is an issue with your son, Jordan, we need to discuss." Tom picked up Sheila and headed directly to the school office where they were ushered into the principal's office. "Tom and Sheila you know how much we love your boys and Nathan is quite the star athlete for us. But there is something I need to share with you now and there is no easy way to say it, so I'm just going to come right out and tell you. It's a school policy to have law enforcement come through on a periodic basis with drug sniffing dogs to see if there are illegal drugs on our campus. The dogs pointed the officers to Jordan's locker and when we opened it we found illegal drugs in it. When we brought Jordan in he didn't deny that they were his. He is sitting in the next room and has been suspended from school."

Obviously, this news hit Tom and Sheila like a ton of bricks. "We had no idea." She exclaimed. "We knew he wasn't into sports or church anymore, but we certainly didn't think he was doing drugs. We wouldn't be so shocked if it was drinking. . . but drugs? That is really hard for us to imagine or accept." Thankfully, with the school's help Tom and Sheila were able to get Jordan into a drug recovery program which he faithfully attended for six weeks. During that time Jordan began going to his church youth group again and when he completed the recovery program, he was able to reenter high school. It seemed as if the situation had been handled and that it had become a one-time episode for Jordan. He completed his junior year and was well into his senior year before another fateful night occurred for Tom and Sheila.

"This is the police department and we need you to come down to the station as soon as possible. Your son was in an accident and while everyone is okay, his blood alcohol level is beyond the legal limit and we found marijuana in his car so we are booking him for DUI and drug possession."

"Are you kidding me?" Tom yelled to Sheila. "What's going on? I thought he was done with that stuff. How did we not see this coming? What are we doing wrong?" Those questions and many more like them would haunt Tom and Sheila for the following months as they traversed yet another drug recovery program with their son. Little did they know that this was only the beginning. Over the course of the next two years Jordan would be in and out of treatment programs where he would "get well" only to fall back into drug use again culminating with the hardest decision Tom and Sheila had to make—to send Jordan to a nine-month treatment program in Utah where they would have little or no contact with him for weeks at a time. "I remember wondering if Jordan was going to make it," Tom recalls. "Each time he came home I would be filled with hope thinking this was it, only to have those hopes dashed time and time again.

Each time I found myself getting angrier and angrier with him and the disease he was battling. Finally, I had to realize that God said we are to forgive not seven times, but seventy times seven (see Matthew 18:20-22), so I committed myself to forgiving him as many times as I needed to so that he could always have another chance because we serve a God of endless second chances."

* *

Faith@Home Family Insight

Tom and Sheila didn't enable Jordan's behavior to continue. They confronted it each time, standing their ground and requiring Jordan to get treatment. At the same time they forgave Jordan and welcomed him home with open arms giving him every opportunity to "leave his life of sin." Unfortunately, as is the case in many households today, getting the individual to leave a life of sin takes multiple attempts and modern Faith@ Home families will grant their children as many chances as it takes.

* *

The highs and lows of this long journey became incredibly difficult for Tom and Sheila and their marriage, yet there were three critical things that helped them get through it. "I can tell you without hesitation," Sheila shared, "that we would not have made it through without our church, our youth pastor and our small group." During the difficult years Tom and Sheila actually became more involved in their church than they had ever previously been. Their son, Nathan, stayed involved in the youth group. That kept them in touch with the youth pastor who was continually in the loop regarding what was going on with Jordan. On numerous occasions the youth pastor would go with Nathan, Tom and Sheila to visit Jordan at the treatment centers he was in. "What I love about our youth pastor is the fact that he never judged Jordan or us for that matter." Tom shared, "He simply took the journey with us and he showed us that God never leaves us. It taught Jordan that you don't have to be perfect to be a part of the church. Here he was in his second, third, fourth rehab unit and our youth pastor just kept coming to see him and hang out with him. I don't know about you but I think that's how Jesus would do it!"

Tom and Sheila had joined a small group from their church which was made up of three other couples who all had teenagers struggling through different kinds of issues. "I love our small group!" Sheila shared excitedly "We don't hide anything and we discuss everything and while at times it seemed like we were always the ones in the most distress, they didn't care. We simply loved one another through the times when we had no answers."

And finally, Tom and Sheila became avid worshippers who hardly missed a Sunday no matter what was going on with Jordan. "We realized we simply needed to be with God more if we were going to get through this," Tom shared. "I wish I could tell you the number of times I didn't want to go because I was either too defeated or embarrassed. Yet it would seem like those were the Sundays when I would get the most out of the worship service. Many times it seemed like the pastor had a camera in our home and that he was preaching directly to me."

. . . .

Faith@Home Family Insight

Tom and Sheila did not turn from the church or other Christians during their times of trial. Instead they turned toward the church and her people! Instead of being ashamed or embarrassed, they became transparent and allowed God to work through His bride, the church, to give them strength and hope for the journey.

. . . .

It seems as if in today's world we feel we cannot air our dirty laundry anywhere and especially, at church. Jesus says, "Come to me, all who are weary and heavy burdened, and I will give you rest. Take my yoke upon you and learn from me, for I am gentle and humble in heart, and you will find rest for your souls" (Matthew 11:27-28). Modern Faith@Home families realize that God is gentle and humble in heart, which means He understands your hurts and he wants to take those burdens from you and replace them with peace so you can rest. What keeps parents awake more, or stirs our hearts more, is when our kids are battling something that we seemingly can do nothing about. But there *is* something we can do. We can go to the one who can do something about it. Nothing is too great for God! So instead of turning away from God out of embarrassment or a sense of feeling defeated, turn towards Him and give Him a chance to do something about the problem. When in a time of trial with your kids . . . worship! When in a time of trial . . . connect and spend time with fellow followers of Christ! And when in a time of trial . . . give your pastor a chance to be a part of your journey. Don't turn from God. Turn toward him!

The Rest of the Story

When Jordan returned from rehab in Utah, he was greeted by his parents, his former youth pastor and a few people he didn't know who said they were a part of some small group with his parents. They said they had been praying for him. Jordan got his GED, attended technical college and got a job as a sound and video technician at a nearby television station. A few years later Jordan started volunteering at the church as a sound technician where he met his wife who was singing in the worship team. They now have two children and Jordan has been sober for over fifteen years. When asked what did it for him Jordan simply said, "My parents, the church and God never gave up on me. They didn't judge me and they always welcomed me back with open arms."

DISCUSSION QUESTIONS

1. Did you ever have a time when you strayed like Jordan? Who was there for you?

2. Has there ever been a time when you have felt too embarrassed or defeated to go to church?

3. What struggles have you or are you facing with your kids today?

4. Who do you need to turn to so that God can give you strength and peace?

3

Turning Battles into Blessings

Dave never envisioned that he would be a caregiving husband. He married his college sweetheart and for the first 20 years of their marriage they had a healthy relationship. Together they brought two wonderful girls into the world and they raised them in a strong Christian home. Dave had a successful business which allowed his wife, Tammy, to be a stay-at-home mom who spent her time shuttling their active daughters from one activity to another. They were active in their church, attending services pretty much every Sunday and Dave was involved in the men's ministry while Tammy volunteered to help in the Sunday School program.

During a lunch meeting Dave confided in his pastor that as a result of a car accident Tammy was going through a difficult battle with a physical ailment. She was in chronic pain. In order to function, Tammy began taking a regimen of pain medications. Over time those medications became less and less effective.

Dave and Tammy went from one specialist to another seeking help and yet each appointment led to disappointment as no clear condition could be identified. All Tammy had to rely on was the pain medication.

Tammy began to battle depression that made it difficult for her even to get out of bed in the morning. Dave and Tammy invited the pastor over on numerous occasions for prayer and they even went to healing centers seeking some sort of miraculous healing from the Lord; yet the pain continued. For periods of time Tammy would get relief for which they would give God thanks and praise, only to see it come back again. That only increased her depression and inability to do the things she wanted to do.

As their daughters began to reach the teenage years they started to question why their mom had to suffer so much and why the doctors couldn't find what was wrong. They even began to question their faith in God wondering how a supposedly good God could sit idly by while their mom suffered. Dave remembers the day when his daughters refused to get ready for church. He went into their room and said, "What's going on? Why aren't you getting ready for church?" To which his daughters responded, "We aren't going to church until God does something to make Mom better. We can't worship and praise a God who allows Mom to be in so much pain." Dave didn't know what to say so he simply said, "I understand because I'm looking for answers to those same questions." You can stay home with Mom while I go.

· ·

Faith@Home Family Insight

Sometimes the best thing we can say is, "I under-stand." We need to alow our children to have their feelings and misgivings and not force them to be in the same place we are.

· ·

On the ride to church Dave cried out to God, "Where are you God? Why aren't you helping? Do you really want my wife to suffer? Do you really want my kids to lose faith in you? Why aren't you doing something? What do you want from me? What am I supposed to do? Just tell me and I will do it. I don't want my wife to suffer and I don't want my kids to walk away from you, but I don't know what to do or say. Give me something, anything. Please Lord."

· ·

Faith@Home Family Insight

It's okay to cry out to God. Don't feel like you need to hold this in or figure it out yourself. Give it to God. Give it all to Him. Don't hold back and don't worry that you will offend God. He's a big God. He can handle it.

· ·

As he walked into church the pastor noticed that Dave was alone so he came over and said, "So you're flying solo today?" "Yeah," Dave responded, "But not by my own choice. Tammy is not well enough to come and my daughters are fed up with her pain and suffering so they are fasting from church until God does something about it." "Well that's a new one." His pastor responded. "Yeah, I didn't really know what to say or do so I just figured it was best to let them do their thing while I did mine." His pastor looked at him with a smile and said, "Well I think you are going to see why God has you here today when you hear the message and that's all I'm going to say."

Dave sat in worship and sang the songs but there was emptiness in his heart because of his concern over his wife and daughters and the fact that he had no idea how to help them. When it came time for the message the pastor came out and said, "Friends, I'm so glad you are here today because we have a special treat for you. We have a guest speaker who is going to share the message today, so would you please join me in welcoming Nick Vujicic[1] to our church." As people applauded Dave looked to see who was coming to preach but all he saw was two men who were setting up a table on the stage. Not knowing what was happening, he wondered to himself if the message was going to be delivered by a magician! The two men left the platform and in came Nick Vujicic, who climbed up on the table. Dave couldn't believe his eyes, as on the table stood a man with no arms or legs. Nick required a table to speak from so people could see him. Dave couldn't take his eyes off Nick as he had never seen a man with no limbs before.

Over the next 45 minutes Nick delivered a riv-eting message about how God had given him the strength to persevere through a lifetime of trials and suffering. Against all odds Nick had taught himself how to become a self-sufficient person. Nick showed a video clip of his morning routine and what he has to go through to get ready for each day including how he brushes his teeth and hair. At the end of his message Nick challenged the entire congregation that they could move beyond their worldly limita-tions to places they never imagined possible so long as they did not give up or turn from God.

At one point, Dave recalls Nick saying, "I still pray that God will give me legs and arms, which I know he can do, and will one day do for me. And then after I pray that prayer, I look down to see if I have legs or arms and when I don't I simply say . . . 'okay then Lord, since that's not your will for me today, then please bless me and use me in a way that is better than a life with arms or legs. '" He then said, "And guess what? God has never let me down. My days are amazing. I've even been on Oprah! How many of you can say that? So I love my life! In fact my life is way better than yours! Have any of you been on Oprah?"

As the audience laughed Nick looked into the group as he prepared to conclude his message. Dave recalls, "His eyes seemed to focus directly on me." Then Nick said, "Are you losing hope? God hears you. He knows your pain. He's here to rescue you. Romans 15:13 says, 'May the God of hope fill you with all joy and peace as you trust in Him, so that you may overflow with hope by the power of the Holy Spirit.'"

As Dave heard those words tears rolled down his face. He now knew the message he needed to take home to his wife and children. He realized it was okay to continually pray for his wife to be healed, and yet he could also pray for more; he could pray for hope and a life filled with purpose and joy that would overwhelm the pain and suffering they faced. He realized that his prayers had been too small and that he needed to start praying for God to work through their ailments to do something in their lives that was even greater than being healed.

As Dave recalls, "As I listened to Nick I actually started to feel jealous of him. How crazy is that? I was jealous of a man with no limbs! That's when I realized that if God can make a man with no limbs say, 'I love my life,' he can certainly do that for us as well."

* *

Faith@Home Family Insight

Dealing with chronic pain, suffering, cancer, or any form of longterm illness can cause all sorts of problems for families. Yet modern Faith@Home families give those conditions to God asking Him to use them to do an even greater work in and through them than could have happened without these conditions. And with God's help these negative situations become blessings.

* *

Dave went home with a video copy of Nick's message. He gathered his family around and said, "There is something I want you to see." They watched Nick's message together. When they were done, Dave led his entire family in a time of prayer where they prayed for more than healing. They prayed for hope. From that day on, as Dave recalls, "everything changed."

The Rest of the Story

Tammy continues to have ups and downs with her suffering, yet the family has hope, peace and joy. Both of their daughters stayed committed to following Christ. One became a physical therapist and the other a nurse and both attribute their mother's condition and the way she handled it as the primary reason why they entered into the professions that they did. Tammy and Dave also launched a ministry in their church called "Courageous Suffering" where people who battle chronic pain can gather for prayer and support. "This has been the greatest blessing in our lives!" Tammy shared, "I love being with these people as their strength and courage builds me up every time we gather together. I think we get more out of the group than anyone else."

In my last conversation with Dave he shared the following with me, "I still pray every day for my wife to be healed and pain free. But I must confess that I'm okay when it doesn't happen because in many ways our lives are better and more fruitful now than when we didn't have this condition. God has taken us to a better place with the pain than I ever envisioned could be possible."

DISCUSSION QUESTIONS

1. What roadblocks did your family face as you grew up?
2. How did you overcome them?
3. What are the roadblocks your family is facing today?
4. How can you pray bigger prayers so that God can help you move beyond them?

Note
1. Read more about Nick Vujicic, the founder of Life Without Limbs, at www.lifewithoutlimbs.org.

4

Your Music Is Driving Me Crazy

José loved his son and enjoyed taking him to ball games, Disneyland, the beach and long hikes in the area hillsides. Both José and his wife Maria worked, so their son, Antonio, attended a church day care program. On his way to work in the morning, José would take Antonio to day care. Maria would pick him up in the afternoon. José loved taking his son to day care as it became a special bonding time for them. "I remember listening to different kids, worship CDs and singing the songs with Antonio on the way to day care. Neither of us could sing very well, but we didn't care because no one could hear us and that just made us sing all the louder!"

Antonio went to Sunday School and would bring home CDs of songs he learned in Sunday School or at Vacation Bible School. José and Antonio would sing those songs in the truck each morning. For a while Antonio was a part of the church choir, but as he got older he began to lose interest and instead of forcing him to continue, José and his wife decided that it was okay if he stopped attending. "It's not like either of us were music majors or anything," Maria stated. "We just figured that the music thing was for a season and now he would get into something else."

As Antonio entered junior high he continued to like music but his musical tastes definitely began to change. "I remember hearing this awful noise coming from his room, like someone screaming while another person ran their fingers down a chalkboard, and I remembered thinking to myself, what in the world is this?" José recollects. "We figured it would just be for a season. Heck, I remember getting into AC/DC when I was about his age and when I told my mom that I wanted an AC/DC High Voltage album for Christmas she went to the electronics department at Sears looking for it because she thought it was some sort of electronic device! It was just a phase I was going through at the time."

Well to their surprise, Antonio's love for the music he liked didn't go away; instead it grew and with it so did his love for the attire and behavior that went with it. "All of a sudden, or so it seemed, he was now wearing dark shirts with dark pants and a dark jacket. He began hanging around with shady looking people," Maria shared. "His grades began to drop and his behavior became more and more disrespectful. In many ways it felt like we were losing our son to the dark side."

Not knowing what to do, and remembering the good times he and his son had listening to music as they drove to day care and school together, José decided he would try something. While Antonio was at school,

José went into his bedroom and grabbed three of his CDs. Then he headed to his Christian bookstore. He went to the music area where an employee greeted and said, "Can I help you?" José handed the employee the CDs and said, "This is the type of music my son has gotten into. I have no idea what it is, but I don't like what it's doing to him. Would you happen to have any Christian music that sounds similar to this?" The employee took a CD out of its case and put it into a CD player. They listened to the first song. He then did the same with the other two CDs.

• •

Faith@Home Family Insight

God works in mysterious ways. Planting seeds in the early years will lead to fruit in the later years. Even though he couldn't sing and had never experienced singing in his family while growing up, José introduced his son to Christian music at an early age through the CDs they would listen to and sing with every day. Through that God planted a seed that would bear fruit in the future.

• •

"This gives me a good idea of the type of music your son is into. Give me a minute and let me go see what I can find," said the employee to José. As José waited he walked over to the area where the children's music was and saw some of the CDs he and Antonio had listened to and remembered those wonderful days when they would sing in the car together on the way to school. He then prayed a simple prayer, "God, you used music to bond us together and now music is tearing us apart, would you please use it to bring us back together again?"

The employee came back holding three CDs, and when he handed them to José, José's initial reaction was, "Are you sure these are Christian? They look just as dark and scary as my son's CDs."

"That's the point," said the employee and then he opened one of them and put it in the CD player and hit play. "When the first song started playing I couldn't believe what I was hearing" exclaimed José, "It was just as crappy sounding to me as the other stuff! But then I opened the CD case and started reading the words and they were powerful. Through this noise the songs were proclaiming how Christ can help you overcome the darkness in your life. While I didn't like the music I did like the words!"

José bought the CDs and the next morning when he was taking Antonio to school he said, "Hey Antonio, I picked up some new music that I really like. Would you mind if I turned it on?" "Are you kidding me, Dad?" Antonio responded, "I don't want to listen to some old Christian songs, sung by a kid's choir. I'm past that." "I know you are," said José, "and I'm not into that anymore either, but I have gotten into something new so I just thought I would run it by you. No big deal. We don't have to. We can just talk instead."

José really knew what he was doing because he also knew his son hated the idea of having to talk all the way to school. Instantly Antonio said, "No that's fine. I'd rather listen to some old school 80s hair-band-sounding music than talk, so go ahead and play it." At that moment José cranked up the volume and hit play and as he recalls, "You should have seen the look on my son's face! I still hated the sound of the song but the look on my son's face made it all worth it."

"Who is this?" Antonio asked.

"It's some new Christian band that has come out recently," José responded.

"This is a Christian band?" Antonio asked with a look of astonishment on his face.

"That's what the guy at the Christian bookstore told me," José replied.

"Not bad," said Antonio, "Not bad at all."

When they pulled into the school parking lot José looked at Antonio and said, "Son you know I love you and always will, but I have noticed that you have begun to change since you've gotten into the kind of music you are listening to now. I can tell you like that style of music, so I'm not here to judge. I took three of your CDs and went to the Christian bookstore and asked them if they had any Christian music that was in this genre and to my surprise they did, so I bought it for you. These CDs are now yours. My hope and prayer is that you will give them a chance so that you can still enjoy the music you like but through it you will also stay connected to God."

Antonio looked at his dad and said, "While I'm not happy that you went into my room and took three of my CDs, I must say that what you did was pretty cool. I'll give them a listen to when I get home from school. Thanks, Dad."

• •

Faith@Home Family Insight

Instead of trying to change our kids, sometimes the best thing we can do is to enter into their world and reality because as we get to know that better, we will get to know them better. The better we understand them, the easier it will be to know what we need to do to influence them. Don't be afraid of their reality. Embrace it and engage in it.

• •

The Rest of the Story

A few weeks later Antonio asked his parents if he could start taking guitar lessons. They gladly agreed. Just two years later Antonio started a band with a few of his friends called "Clanging Symbol." Together they made a joyful noise playing their brand of Christian music for their youth group and other youth groups in the area who invited them to come and play. The band never made it big. In fact it was only together for a few years until the members all went separate ways. Antonio went to college and is now a youth pastor who still enjoys playing a unique brand of Christian music whenever he has the opportunity to do so. "I don't know where I would be now had it not been for what my dad did for me when I was in junior high," recalls Antonio. "All I know is that I certainly wouldn't be where I am today. What my dad did was crazy, but it was a crazy cool. He didn't try to change me. Instead he guided me towards the right path based on who I was and what I was into."

DISCUSSION QUESTIONS

1. What did you do growing up that shocked your parents, or at least pushed their boundaries a little bit?
2. How did they handle it? What did they do well or not so well? What do you wish they would have done?
3. What "world" do you need to enter into to know your children better?
4. What scares you about that world? What are some ways you can positively influence your kids as they navigate through that world?

5

Not How I Expected It to Be

Lydia never imagined that she would be a single mom. She got married after college to a man she had fallen in love with and dated for two years prior to getting married. They started life together while both were active professionals in the companies where they worked. After three years of married life they decided to have children and over the next four years they gave birth to a son and two daughters. Lydia worked part time while her husband, Stan, continued to work full time. Everything seemed to be going well for them although Stan's hours and travels seemed to be steadily increasing. Due to the stress and time commitments of trying to raise three kids under the age of five and hold down two jobs, Lydia and Stan didn't have much time to maintain their relationship. It began to suffer as a result.

Stan and Lydia began to fight and that caused Stan to stay away from home more which only made things worse. About a year later Stan came home from work and told Lydia that he no longer loved her. He had fallen in love with someone at work and he would be filing for a divorce. The next year was very painful as Lydia juggled working, being a mom, the divorce, the sale of their home and a move to a new, much smaller home.

Faith@Home Family Insight

We live in a world that always makes us wish and want for what we don't have. This keeps us on a constant quest for more and yet when we become parents we must pause from this quest for more in lieu of making parenting our highest priority. Therefore, instead of wishing for a different reality, we need to take the reality we have and make it the very best faith at home environment it can be for our children. I was raised in a rundown mobile home that, compared to the homes where my friends were raised, would have looked like we were living in poverty. Yet, as I look back on my life, I don't even remember "home" as a mobile home. I remember it as the greatest place, with some of the greatest food, fun and laughter—because my parents made it that way. Don't worry if you don't seem to have the greatest worldly place or situation. God can make it better than any mansion on this earth!

"I was pretty much the crazy one," Lydia recalls. "I had to keep all the plates spinning while Stan could come swooping in, pick up the children for a day and take them to do fun things. When he was done he would simply dump them back on me and say, 'Good luck! Look forward to seeing them next week.'"

Prior to the divorce Stan and Lydia attended church as time allowed. "We weren't C & E'rs (Christmas and Easter attendees) but we also weren't regular attendees either. We just went to church when it would work for us to go, but we certainly weren't active participants," Lydia recalled. After the divorce was over and everything had settled somewhat for Lydia, she knew she needed help in how to be a single mom but she didn't know where to turn to. "Here I am a woman in my mid thirties trying to hold down a job and raise three kids on my own. This was not how I pictured it would be, but this was where I was. I figured, like it or not, I need to hunker down and do this, and do it well, because I'm all these three kids have."

Lydia had two friends who were constantly inviting her to come to church with them. She didn't really want to go because she felt church was for "perfect families" and she and her kids were certainly not a perfect family. She allowed her kids to go to Vacation Bible School and they came home every day super excited to share things that had happened. Their stories began to warm Lydia's heart. At the end of the Vacation Bible School week the parents were invited to attend a closing celebration where the children sang their favorite VBS songs followed by a slide show depicting things they had done over the course of the week. At the end of the program the children's ministry leader thanked the parents for allowing their kids to be a part of VBS, and then she said the following: "We know that for some of you this is the first time you have done anything at our church. You let your kids come and for that we want to say thank you. If your kids had a good time we would like you to know that we have something coming for you parents. You see, we don't want VBS to be the end of the good times. We want to help you continue to have fun times like this in your home with your kids. And we know that some of you sitting here today like that idea but you are probably thinking, *I'm too busy for that or I'm not trained to do that or I certainly don't have the perfect home so I'm probably not qualified for that either.* To that we simply want to say that you *do* have time because we are going to show you how to have fun times through things you are already doing. You are qualified because you are their parent. So all we want to do is to help show you how easily you can have fun with your kids in your home." Lydia looked around because a part of her thought they were saying this directly to her. Then she realized this was simply an open invitation to anyone. She grabbed the postcard with the information and put it in her purse and headed home with her children.

Over the course of the next few days, Lydia remembers, "That postcard kept popping up. I swear I threw it away three times, but I kept finding it on the table, next to the refrigerator, or on the floor. I finally succumbed and decided to go." Lydia was nervous as she was afraid she would be the only single parent in the room. She worried that the program would promote parents needing to spend an hour a day with their children, sitting quietly at the kitchen table with a candle burning and having some sort of deep Bible study or family devotions. She knew that in her house, with her children, there would be no chance of success.

....

Faith@Home Family Insight

Satan is going to tell you all sorts of lies to keep you from giving God, and His ways, a chance. Don't listen to those lies! Give God a chance and you will find yourself saying, "Why did I get so worried about this?" Remember, God wants to help life go well for you and your family.

....

As she waited for the event to begin, she literally found herself getting so nervous that she began to pack up and leave, but just before she could, the children's pastor came to the front of the room and said, "Are there any perfect parents here today? Anyone here got it all together? Anyone got the perfect family? Perfect kids? Perfect home environment? Because if you do, you need to leave right now because this seminar is not for you. This seminar is for imperfect parents, with imperfect families and imperfect home environments." Lydia recalls, "She had me at that point!"

The seminar focused on how to have fun "God moments" with your kids at home and it identified four "times" when it could happen: mealtime, morning time, bedtime and car time.

• •

Faith@Home Family Insight

Deuteronomy 6:7 identifies four opportunities that God provides every day for us to weave faith talk, prayer and Bible reading into our daily lives. "Impress them on your children. Talk about them when you sit at home and when you walk along the road, when you lie down and when you get up." Modern Faith@ Home families take advantage of these times.

• •

"I learned at the seminar, that those four times happen every day," Lydia recalled. "So instead of thinking I needed to find time for some sort of family devotions—which I clearly do not have time for—I learned instead that I can simply take advantage of these four times that occur every day."

The seminar went on to showcase ways parents could engage in prayer, Bible reading or faith talk with their kids in the car, at bedtime, in the morning or at mealtime. "I was blown away with how easy it was," Lydia shared "Don't get me wrong, I wasn't doing any of them at the time but when I walked out of the room

I knew exactly how I could bring God into our crazy home life, so that's what I did." Over the course of the next year Lydia decided to take advantage of those times. She made sure someone would always pray at mealtime. She used car time as a chance to listen to Christian CD's with songs the kids could sing, and then as the kids got older she found a CD that would read a Scripture passage each day on the way to school. The kids would listen to it and together discuss what it meant. "Another thing we came up with for the ride to school was what we called the *look out!* prayer. On occasion I would simply yell, *look out!* And when I did everyone would have to be silent and look out a different window of the car. Of course I would look out the front window, and for the next two minutes we would look for things that God would bring to our attention to pray for or about. Then, when the two minutes were up we would simply go from person to person praying for the things we saw."

At bedtime Lydia began to pray with her children or read a story Bible with them. She said, "Nighttime was always a little tricky with three kids because each one of them is different and some nights I would do three different things with three different kids while other nights we would all gather and do it together. It really didn't matter to me."

What Lydia found to be most effective in the morning was a simple blessing that she would say over each of her kids before they left the home. The blessing was taught to her at the seminar and was based on

Numbers 6:24-26, "May the Lord bless you and keep you. May the Lord make His face shine on you and be gracious to you. May the Lord look upon you with favor and give you peace. In the name of the Father, and the Son and the Holy Spirit. Amen."

Faith@Home Family Insight

We were all created uniquely which means we must recognize that everyone is going to have a different way for how they best connect with God. Don't force your children to do it your way. Accept them for who they are and adapt to what works best for them. I was not a morning person so trying to have some sort of faith talk with me in the morning would not have worked well which is why my mom left me alone in the mornings. But I was a night owl and a lot of times my mom would wait till everyone was off to bed before she would enter into some sort of faith talk with me. I never had a problem doing faith talk with her because I didn't want to go to bed anyway!

The Rest of the Story

As her children have grown Lydia has continued to take advantage of car time, bed time, morning time and mealtime to keep God in the center of her family's life. "Before that seminar I thought God was someone you visited at church" Lydia recalls, "I never imagined God could be a permanent resident in our home." The ways of engaging in faith talk, prayer, Bible reading etc. have changed as the kids have grown older. Lydia has taken advantage of Bible apps and recently she found one that is a Bible reading program which everyone has on their cell phone and it alerts the other members of the family when someone has completed their reading for the day. "I know how competitive we are as a family, so I knew that a Bible reading app would be the one that works best for us" Lydia shared with excitement. "Unfortunately, I'm usually the last one to get it done and now everyone knows it!"

Lydia still lives in the same little house with her three teenage daughters. To this point, has not remarried, but as she shared with me, "We have the greatest house in the world, not because it's the biggest or nicest, which it clearly isn't, but it's the best because Christ resides here with us!"

DISCUSSION QUESTIONS

1. What was the spiritual environment in your home growing up? Did faith talk, prayer or Bible reading happen in your home?
2. Which are you better at; faith dialogue, prayer or Bible reading? Which do your kids prefer?
3. What "times" work best for you; bed time, meal time, morning time, car time?
4. How have you, or can you, engage in faith talk, prayer or Bible reading at bed time, meal time, morning time, or car time?

6

Balancing When Imbalanced

A youth pastor shared the following with me.

When I got into youth ministry I was excited to reach students for Christ and to help them become fully devoted followers of Him. I had grown up in a Christian family and church was pretty much part of my DNA. I attended a Christian college, majored in religion and was involved in a variety of ministry teams that would go on mission trips or lead youth retreats for area church youth groups. Every summer I worked at a Bible camp and I always knew that I was going to be a youth pastor because I loved working with students. After college, and a few years in camping ministry, I was hired as a youth pastor and I began reaching and discipling students. I led youth group, took kids to camp, organized mission trips and even let the kids color my hair at a lock in. I was your typical young, cool, fun and engaging youth pastor.

I knew when I got into youth ministry that I would be faced with difficult situations like teens doing drugs and alcohol, Internet pornography and bad home environments with absent or disengaged parents. I knew that we would have some kids who would be coming from strong Christian households where faith was a part of their life while others would be street kids who had never encountered anything to do with Christ before. I knew I would face teenagers who would challenge me, reject me make fun of me, but who would also love and follow me. I was not naïve as I had studied adolescent behaviors in college and had worked with hundreds of kids at Bible camps, so I felt pretty prepared to handle just about anything. I was even somewhat prepared to handle the phone call I received late one night telling me that one of the students in our youth group had been killed in a car accident. I went to the hospital, cried with the parents. I gathered the rest of the students in our youth room at church, so they had a safe place to mourn and even cry out in anger. And I lead a difficult funeral service that through God's grace brought comfort and hope to family and friends who gathered to mourn the loss of their loved one.

But there was one thing for which I was ill prepared. At first there weren't many cases of it but as the years rolled on I started to see it more and more frequently. In fact, by my tenth year in ministry it was clearly the biggest issue I faced in youth ministry and that was chemical imbalances like depression, anxiety, ADD, ADHD, etc.

Jimmy was one of the "fringe" kids in my youth group and in spite of the fact that he didn't come from a Christian home, Jimmy was a regular at youth group and he had a special bond with me. A lot of nights Jimmy would hang around after youth group and help clean up. Many times I would drive Jimmy home. One night as I was driving Jimmy home, I noticed he was a little more amped up than normal and he seemed to be rubbing his arm a lot.

"What's up with your arm?" I asked Jimmy. "Nothing" Jimmy responded. "C'mon. I can tell something's wrong with it what did you do? Did you hurt is skateboarding?" I asked. "No. It's nothing like that." Jimmy responded. "Then what is it?" I asked again. "I cut my arm." Jimmy said timidly. "What do you mean you cut your arm? Did you cut it doing something?" I inquired, not knowing what would come out of Jimmy's mouth next. "I cut it a bunch of times just because

I felt like cutting it." Jimmy shared. "Let me see it." I said. Jimmy rolled up his sleeve to reveal the dozens of cuts across his arm. I knew I had to tell Jimmy's parents and over the course of the next few weeks Jimmy was diagnosed as being manic depressive with suicidal tendencies.

Elizabeth was an athletic teenager who excelled in track and cross country. She came from a solid Christian home and was one of the silent but strong members of our youth group. She got good grades and was pretty much the type of teen that seemed to have it all together. During her sophomore year, Elizabeth began to put on a little weight and as a result her times in cross country began to slow. Her parents thought this was normal for a teen girl going through puberty, so they didn't think much of it. As the year continued Elizabeth's grades began to drop and yet the parents attributed it to the fact that she was taking advanced, college prep courses which were more difficult. Then, when track season came around, Elizabeth really began to struggle. She become more agitated and frustrated with her coaches, she lashed out at her parents more and one night her parents got a call from the parents of her best friend where she was spending the night. They had just found the two girls passed out with alcohol bottles next to them. The parents called me and when I showed up it looked like a bomb had gone off in their room. I couldn't believe that two girls this young and little could drink as much as they did and survive. It was clearly a cry for help. Thankfully, both girls were okay, but shortly thereafter Elizabeth was diagnosed as having anxiety.

I could share one example after another of teenagers in my youth group who had chemical imbalances that they had to do battle with. When I started in youth ministry, I might have one or two students who would be on medication and I would need to monitor them when I took them to camp or on a retreat. Now I have to take a nurse or dedicated person with me whose sole responsibility is to keep track of the medications and make sure each student takes it as prescribed. I would guess that it's somewhere between a third and a half of the students in my youth group are on medication for some type of chemical imbalance.

Over the years I have come alongside literally hundreds of families who have children with chemical imbalances and through those experiences I saw how some families navigated it well while others did not do so well. As a result of those experiences

I identified some key principles that successful families used to navigate their way through these difficult years.

• •

Faith@Home Family Insight

Chemical imbalances are real and cannot be ignored. Modern Faith@Home families recognize this and do not shy away from getting these imbalances diagnosed and treated. They also make sure their children understand that these imbalances are not caused by God, but they are result of original sin. God can and will provide them the ability to overcome these imbalances if they continually put their faith and trust in Him.

• •

1. Raise Awareness So as to Take Away Any Shame or Embarrassment

I noticed that the families who handled chemical imbalances well were families that became very knowledgeable about the condition they were facing. A lot of stereotypes exist around chemical imbalances and many of them are dead wrong. The families that seemed to handle their condition well were families who were ruthless at learning about their condition to the point that they would even find other people and families who had similar conditions. They joined some sort of small group or found a way to consistently network with a small group.

. . . .

Faith@Home Family Insight

Get well versed in your child's condition and find others who have faced a similar imbalance. Establish
some sort of ongoing relationship with them for ongoing support and advice.

. . . .

2. Place the Blame Where the Blame Belongs

I also noticed that these families made sure their children understood that God did not cause their condition, but that He was there to give them what they
needed to battle through it. Some families didn't
know what to say about God as they watched their
child fight a chemical imbalance. This caused ongoing issues for their child and his/her relationship
with God. The Faith@Home families seemed to make
sure that their children did not blame God for their
imbalances. Instead they were diligent in making
sure their kids understood that Satan and sin were
responsible, not God.

3. Make It Easy to Talk About

I also noticed that the families who navigated their
chemical imbalance journeys well seemed to be very
open about it. They didn't hide it under the rug, they
didn't pretend it didn't exist; in fact they made it seem
as normal as having the flu. For some reason, while
chemical imbalances are prevalent in our society

today, talking about them still isn't. If someone has cancer we talk openly about it. We surround them with support groups and prayer, yet, when someone is diagnosed with a bipolar condition it seems that many people turn away because they don't know what to say or do. Modern Faith@Home families understand that while they cannot change society, they can make sure their home environment is a safe, secure and open place for children with chemical imbalances to discuss their condition and how it impacts their day and life. Many families I know came up with a unique name for their child's condition. For example, one family simply called it "Bi" as in "Bye" so they would simply ask their son, "How's your Bi today?" It was a way they could talk about it openly without it making it a big deal.

4. Jump in the Roller Coaster Car with Them

Another reality of a chemical imbalance is that it puts the individual and his or her family on a roller coaster ride of ups and downs—good days and bad days, medications that work and medications that don't. It's an ever changing thing because our chemicals, bodies and environments are always changing. The families who handle it well are families where the parents jump into the roller coaster with their child. They take the ride with them rather than watching them saying, "I hope they make it." Anyone who knows someone who has a chemical imbalance knows it is an ever changing thing and it's a lonely place to be. There is no quick fix for a chemical imbalance, yet modern Faith@Home families realize that their chemical imbalance is simply a part of life, so they deal with it accordingly and adapt as necessary.

5. Trust the Process

The last thing I noticed was the way these families ruthlessly trusted and committed themselves to the treatment process. One of the most difficult aspects of a chemical balance is how hard it is to treat. And not only is it hard to treat, but it requires ongoing treatment that constantly needs to change as well. Each change can take two to three weeks before you know if it has worked or not. It's extremely hard to trust a process that may take two or three weeks to get the results you are looking for, especially when it's your children who are being treated! Yet the families I experienced who navigated these years well seemed to find a way to trust their treatment process. There was one critical component that enabled them to do that. They made sure that their doctor had the full picture of how their child was doing. Doctors can't accurately treat something they don't see or know about. In the same way, doctors who are treating children with chemical imbalances need as much accurate information to work with as possible. Modern Faith@Home families "speak the truth in love" no matter how hard it is for their loved one to hear it and it is especially true for the parents of children with chemical imbalances. They make sure their doctors/counselors have ALL the information so that they have the best chance of helping their child be as healthy as possible.

One of the biggest modern realities that families face today has to do with chemical imbalances of some sort. It could be in the parent or the child but in either case the keys just covered can help you as you "do life" with these imbalances. As you know, "God never leaves you nor forsakes you," and, "He never gives you more than you can handle," which means with HIS help you can overcome these imbalances. Keep learning about them and how others dealt with them successfully. Talk about it openly as a family. Take the ride of treatment together and trust the process by being ruthlessly honest with your caregivers so they can help you.

DISCUSSION QUESTIONS

1. Do you know someone who has battled a chemical imbalance?
2. What are some of the misconceptions or stereotypes that go with chemical imbalances?
3. What prevents families from discussing their chemical imbalances openly with others?
4. What is your reaction to the steps to positively handling chemical imbalances that were listed in this episode?

7

Unequally Yoked

When Yolanda went to church she knew she would be going without her husband. Sunday morning was his time to golf and nothing was going to get in the way of that for him. He also wasn't interested in church because in his opinion, "All they ultimately want is our money." Yolanda and her husband Roland had been married for eight years and they had two children who were six and four years old. "Even though I didn't go to church much when I was growing up, I always felt it would be a good thing for my kids, so that's ultimately why I decided to go." Yolanda's husband was not "anti" church but he wasn't supportive of it either. "Essentially," Yolanda shared, "He said that I could take the kids to church so long as I didn't start pressuring him to go. I figured he was gone golfing all Sunday morning, so I really didn't figure I had anything to lose. I started checking into churches and found one that was nearby with a really good children's ministry program and that's where we went."

When Yolanda and her children arrived at the church the parking lot was filled with activity as people were coming and going. Yolanda got her two children out of the car and they walked towards the entrance to the church. As they neared the entrance a greeter welcomed them and asked if she could help them with anything. "I'm wondering where I take my kids," Yolanda said, "It's our first time here and I would like to get my kids into your Sunday School program." "I would be glad to help" the greeter responded and she led them to the children's ministry area where Yolanda was able to enroll her children in the Sunday School program. "The whole time I was wondering if I was doing the right thing, but everyone seemed nice and the kids didn't cry so I figured it was okay," Yolanda recalled. Yolanda then made her way to the sanctuary where, because of the time it took to get her kids enrolled, she was late for the service. Not wanting to disrupt anything she considered just going to the bookstore and café. Then an usher saw her and said, "Come here, I have a great inconspicuous spot that is open just for you." Yolanda followed him into the sanctuary to the seat he pointed out. She sat down. As she got settled she really wasn't thinking about church much because at this point she felt she had done what she was supposed to do, which was to get her kids into a church program. "I was really doing this for my kids," Yolanda remembers "I just wanted them to have some God in their life and I figured this was the best way to make it happen."

Eventually Yolanda began to pay attention to what was happening in the worship service. A video came on the screens. The words across the video were, "Do you want to get well?" and the video depicted people saying that they wanted to get well followed by all sorts of humorous actions they were engaging in that clearly kept them from getting well. Following the video clip the pastor's message focused on that statement, "Do you want to get well?" Yolanda recalls, "I felt he was preaching directly to me. I knew I wasn't well, or at least not as well as I wanted to be. I knew our marriage wasn't well and neither was our family, but I wasn't ready to admit it to anyone." The pastor talked about how Jesus asked a man, who had been an invalid for 38 years, "Do you want to get well?" The question seemed to have an obvious answer; who doesn't want to get well, right? "The reality," he explained, "is that for many they will say they want to get well and yet don't really want to do what they have to do to get well. Some have given up on thinking it can actually happen.

"That question," Yolanda explained, "is not as obvious as it seems. I was forced to ask myself if I really wanted to get well. Do I want my life, my marriage and my family to be well or am I just going to keep on doing what I've been doing expecting and hoping that someday things will change." The pastor then went on to share the definition of insanity as being, "doing the same thing over and over again yet expecting different results." He said that people do not have to wait to hit rock bottom before they change. Each one of these points sank deeper and deeper into

Yolanda's heart and when the pastor concluded his
sermon by inviting anyone who wanted to get well
to come forward, she literally sprang out of her seat
and came forward, giving her life to Christ for the
very first time.

• •

Faith@Home Family Insight

When you don't know what to do, turn it over to
God asking Him to show you what you need to do
to change/improve your current condition.

• •

Yolanda was so excited, yet she didn't have anyone
she could talk to about it. She tried to explain to her
children what had happened but at four and six years
old it was difficult for them to understand. She knew
she couldn't tell her husband. She didn't think he
would respond favorably. "I could only imagine his
response," Yolanda recalls. "Hey, honey, no big deal
but I thought you should know that I came to the
realization in church today that we aren't well so I
gave my life to Christ and from this day forward I'm
not going to be the same person, our marriage is not
going to be the same nor is our family." So Yolanda
didn't say anything and instead she simply started
to pray a simple prayer to God, "Yes, Lord, I want to
get well and I realize that you love me and my family
and you want to help us. I have committed myself to
doing whatever you need me to do so that I can be

well but I am going to need your help. I need you to show me how to get well because I don't have a clue how to make myself, my marriage or my kids better. I'm scared but I'm putting my faith and trust in you."

The following Sunday Yolanda went to church and the pastor's message again focused on how to get well by following the Deuteronomy 6 roadmap. The pastor's points were pretty straight forward.

1. Know what the commands/ways of God are. If you don't know what they are, commit yourself to learning them.
2. Be careful to obey the commands/ways of God. Obedience is a choice, so just do it!
3. Live "in love" with God where all those around can see that it is a real love that is in your heart, soul and strength.
4. Talk openly about God without expectations and without being ashamed.
5. Remain in love with God; don't let false hopes or expectations lead you away from Him.

Yolanda had been praying for a plan she could follow for the way in which she, her marriage and her family could become well. Now she had her marching orders. She spent the next six months going to church with her kids, learning what the commands and ways of God were. She read books that others recommended to her. She helped her kids with their

Sunday School lessons and even joined a Sunday morning Bible study group that helped her learn even more about God and his ways.

"In many ways I think I learned more from my kids and what they were learning at Sunday School than they did!" she recalled. As she learned the ways of God she also diligently obeyed. For example she learned how to pray with her children and when she did she began praying with them at bedtime and in the car on the way to school. She also learned how a wife is supposed to love, honor and pray for her husband. She began being obedient to those commands. She never once challenged her husband to become a Christian or even attend church with her. She had learned that any change in her husband was ultimately a work that God would have to do in her husband's heart. She surrendered herself to God's will and timing for her husband.

● ●

Faith@Home Family Insight

In an unequally yoked situation, instead of trying to change your spouse, change yourself to be more in love with God and obedient to Him and His ways. We can't control our children or a spouse but we can control ourselves and how we live.

● ●

As Yolanda learned about Christ and what He had done for her on the cross, she found herself falling more in love with Christ. "I mean, how can you not love someone who willingly gave up his life for you?" Yolanda recalls. "And he didn't just do it for me, but for my husband and children as well. He made a pathway through death to eternal life for all of us, so that death, no matter when it comes, will not be the end of our relationship. How great is Jesus!" While Yolanda never pushed Jesus or church on her husband, she also didn't shy away from it either. She listened to Christian music and whenever her husband would ask about the church or anything to do with God she would answer as simply and succinctly as she could. About a year and half later she remembers getting a birthday card from her husband with the following note inside, "I don't know what's happened with you lately but I really appreciate the way you are now. I can tell this God thing has helped you somehow and while I'm not interested in it yet, I do like how it's impacting you and the kids. I just wanted you to know that." Yolanda recalls, "What I remember from that note is one word; YET! When Roland wrote that he wasn't interested in it "yet" I realized that was a step in the right direction and that gave me hope to keep on keepin' on!"

Yolanda kept going to church with her children. She read books and learned how to love her husband and children better. As she learned, she kept applying the things she learned to her behavior and adapted accordingly. When opportunities arose to talk to her husband about God, she did. She invited him to go with them to the Christmas Eve service. He agreed. "It was almost more fearful and exciting for me than our wedding!" Yolanda recalled. Over two years had passed since Yolanda had given her life to Christ, and now her entire family was worshipping together on Christmas Eve! "It took everything I had in me not to cry through the entire service."

The Rest of the Story

Roland was not a quick and easy change. He spent the next three years being a Christmas and Easter church attendee. Yolanda never got discouraged, nor did she change from being a person who was passionately living a life that was clearly in love with Christ. Finally, following a compelling Easter message, Roland decided to take another step by attending a men's gathering that was going to feature a former professional golfer as the guest speaker. "I remember thinking this would be a good way to get an autograph" Roland recalled "because I had a pretty good collection of golf paraphernalia in my office and something autographed by him would be good to add to my collection." What Roland didn't realize would be happening was the "secret weapon" of what his wife and children would do while he went to the men's event; they sat at their kitchen table and prayed for him. "We never brought this golfing event to Roland's attention. He found it listed in the bulletin himself so we figured this might be God's handiwork." Yolanda remembered "As soon as he left I gathered the kids and told them that their Dad was going to a men's event at church. They couldn't believe it. I asked if they wanted to join me in praying for Dad. I thought it would be for a few minutes at most. I didn't expect our prayer time to last the entire 90 minutes until he came home!"

At the men's event the professional golfer shared his testimony. That somehow grabbed Roland's heart and began his change and turn towards God. While it was not nearly as dramatic or as fast as Yolanda's conversion, it became steady nonetheless, leading to a point where a few years later Roland got baptized with his wife and daughters standing next to him. "That was the best day of my life!" Roland recalls. "I still can't believe how patient, and honoring to God, my wife and children were even when I wasn't in it with them. They are the heroes in our story. Not me."

DISCUSSION QUESTIONS

1. How do you react to the statement made by Jesus, "Do you want to get well?"
2. What are some things that prevent you from wanting to get well?
3. Have you ever been in or experienced an unequally yoked situation?
4. How would you assess yourself on the Deuteronomy 6 roadmap to wellness? Which areas need strengthening?

MARK A. HOLMEN

To find out more about Mark Holmen's
speaking engagements and to learn more about
the Faith@Home movement, visit faithathome.com.
Mark is available to speak to parents and church
leaders about how to be a faith-at-home focused
individual, family and church. For more information,
please contact Mark at mark@faithathome.com.